LONG TERM CARE

BRIDGING THE GAP BETWEEN YOU AND EXTENDED CARE

PRESENTED BY
ROY SNARR, CFF®, CLTC®, NSSA®, LACP™

Copyright © 2023 Roy Snarr, CFF®, CLTC®, NSSA®, LACP™

LONG TERM CARE

This publication is designed to provide accurate and authoritative information regarding the subject matter contained within. It should be understood that the author and publisher are not engaged in rendering legal, accounting or other financial service through this medium. The author and publisher shall not be liable for your misuse of this material and shall have neither liability nor responsibility to anyone with respect to any loss or damage caused, or alleged to be caused, directly or indirectly by the information contained in this book. The author and/or publisher do not guarantee that anyone following these strategies, suggestions, tips, ideas, or techniques will become successful. If legal advice or other expert assistance is required, the services of a competent professional should be sought.

Roy Snarr is the author of this book, and the book is presented by Roy Snarr. Roy Snarr is a well-known asset protection expert with over a decade of experience. He has written many articles on annuities, long term care and other financial topics, and has been a featured commentator on TV, Radio, and the Internet.

All rights reserved. No portion of this book may be reproduced mechanically, electronically, or by any other means, including photocopying, without written permission of the author. It is illegal to copy the book, post it to a website, or distribute it by any other means without permission from the author.

The Author can be reached directly at BeyondPublishing.net

Manufactured and printed in the United States of America distributed globally by BeyondPublishing.net

New York | Los Angeles | London | Sydney

ISBN Hardcover: 978-1-63792-988-9
ISBN Softcover: 978-1-63792-553-9

TABLE OF CONTENTS

Foreword: Why I'm Writing This Book — 7

Chapter 1: Medicare DOES Care…About Certain Things — 13

Chapter 2: Long-Term Care Overview — 22

Chapter 3: Understanding the WHY — 30

Chapter 4: LTCi Options — 33

Chapter 5: Medicaid — 36

Chapter 6: Medicare — 38

Chapter 7: Short-Term Plans for LTCi — 42

Chapter 8: Long-Term Care Insurance Payout Options — 44

Chapter 9: Traditional LTCi — 47

Chapter 10: Asset-Based LTCi- Life Insurance and Annuities — 51

Chapter 11: Life Insurance Hybrids — 53

Chapter 12: Annuity-Based LTC — 62

Chapter 13: Tax Advantages — 70

Chapter 14: Handling Self Objections — 72

Chapter 15: Common Long-Term Care Terminology — 77

FOREWORD

WHY I'M WRITING THIS BOOK

I have a passion for helping people. This book will be similar in style to my other book on Social Security, *Guaranteed Monies*. The content comes from my experience in helping thousands of people across the country learn often overlooked financial tactics. I have personally lived through these experiences, and I've set out to help as many people as possible avoid some of the downfalls that my family personally went through. For me, this career is rewarding, because I can touch the lives of so many families and help financially protect them.

Just like Social Security, long-term care planning is often overlooked; nobody wants to talk about it. I don't blame them! Who wants to think about the question, "Who is going to change my diaper in 15-20 years?" Nobody! We would rather talk about all the fun things in life! And I'm right there with you!

However, in the event that you become sick and need assistance, you must have a plan in place. Without a plan, you could potentially run through your entire life savings, sell off assets, and create immense financial and emotional stress on your family. No one wants to put their family through that!

My journey through the financial services world over this last decade (plus) has made me realize that most financial advisors, insurance agents, estate planning attorneys, etc. are not hitting home on the overwhelming fact that long-term care will affect the majority of people – nor are they discussing how expensive it is.

Personally, I have lived through four long-term care situations:

The first was my mother's father who was a WWII veteran. He was a super-tough guy, always self-sufficient, and very stubborn. There is no way he would <u>ever</u> ask for help. However, he was diagnosed with Alzheimer's. It was a painful six-year process for the family, and because of his disease, he didn't know what was going on.

Many people will think the same way as my grandfather did. They'll say, "When I get to that point, I won't burden my family!" Well, unless your family doesn't care about you, then you're going to burden them – not intentionally! But they love you, so they're going to want the best for you. If you don't have anything in place to help them, they will have to come up with the solution themselves.

Keep in mind:

A lot of this planning that we're going to be talking about in this book is a selfless move. You're not necessarily doing it for <u>yourself</u> – you're doing it for the ones you care about. You'll simply have to ask yourself, "Are they worth it?"

If you answered "yes," then let's get to planning.

The next long-term care event that I went through was with my dad's mother. She was an amazing woman who lived to the age of 96 years old! She was always self-sufficient. There are pictures of her smoking cigarettes during the Great Depression!

The last few years of her life, she needed full-time assistance. Luckily, we had a family member who was able to take care of her, which added more funds to support the actual cost. Eventually, when she passed away, we sold her home and property, and used part of the proceeds to pay back the family member who helped take care of her.

We are still very grateful to this day. Without our family members, we don't know what we would have done! There's no way that we would have put the matriarch of our family into some shabby nursing home or state-run assisted living facility. That was not going to happen!

But for many, there is <u>no other option.</u> Many are forced to put their loved ones in some sort of a home, and if you don't have the financial means, it may not be a very nice one. You can think of nursing homes and assisted living facilities as hotels– you can either stay at the five-star Ritz or the Motel 1 on the bad side of town. The goal is to try to get somewhere in the middle, like a three-star hotel, where you can have good care, it's clean, it has a good reputation, and you're not worried about any type of abuse on your family members.

The third long-term care situation was with my mother's mother. My mother had to change her own life to take care of her mother. My grandmother ended up moving into a modular home, and my mother moved next door. My grandmother had a nice piece of property, but was unable to take care of it. The only way to make all the money work was to sell the property.

Over the next few years, she progressively got worse, and it consumed the family's life, because we wanted to do everything possible to ensure that she was comfortable and happy. If we would have had additional money or resources, things would have been easier. We could have had trained professional help. Money isn't everything, but it definitely helps! It is a unique tool that can provide freedom and options.

The fourth and most recent event was my wife's grandfather who lived into his late 90s. He was a fascinating man, and I always enjoyed spending time with him. I remember having the hard conversation with the family when they called me with questions about the coverage for his in-home stay. They were having challenges getting his Medicare plan to pay for everything.

Again, *this* is where the hard conversation happens!

<u>Medicare doesn't cover the majority of long-term care</u>.

There was no other policy in place, so all the money for care had to come directly from his financial accounts. Fortunately, there was not much suffering, and he went quickly. But other people don't have that opportunity. They may be stuck in a long-term care situation for much longer. (In my grandfather's case, he spent six years needing care, and not having much of an idea of what was going on). Others may have the presence of mind to understand what's happening, but continue to suffer with limited resources.

Through all these events, I was either too young to help the family with anything or they were too old for me to help them with any type of insurance. But, as I started learning more about the financial services industry and seeing how this affected my own family, let alone the families of my clients, I decided to dive in 100 percent to long-term care insurance. I wanted to help people explore their options and become educated on the topic.

And that's the whole goal — education.

We offer long-term care solutions as a business, but this business is more than just a job for us — it's about a relationship. We've been blessed to become one of the top-producing long-term care agencies in the entire country, and have consecutively ranked in the top one percent of agencies over the years. I say this in a very humble way to provide relevance and credibility. There's a lot of people out there who are in the financial services space. There are Medicare agents, financial advisors, insurance agents, etc. However, we have found that only a few actually know and understand the value enough to provide long-term care insurance education and solutions.

We will work with you, your family, and your other financial counselors that are part of your portfolio to help you get the best plan available for *you*. This model has created many unique partnerships for us and provides an extra resource for folks just like yourself in retirement.

In my speaking events, I often mention that everyone should have a separation of specialists. You need to have someone who specializes in money management, someone who specializes in Medicare insurance, someone who specializes in taxes/estate planning and <u>someone who specializes in long-term care (LTC) and asset protection</u>.

We are your LTC and asset protection specialists!

If you're reading this book, you've already started making more progress than most people have. By the time you're finished with this book, you'll have a good understanding of long-term care insurance, your options, and most importantly, how those options can be implemented into your personal financial strategy. We work with people across all 50 states and even have international policy options.

Feel free to reach out to us! We are happy to have a conversation to see how we can help. I hope you enjoy the read. I tried to keep it short and brief. There's so much information that we couldn't put into here. The pages to come detail the highlights of long-term care insurance and how to implement it in your life.

CHAPTER 1

MEDICARE DOES CARE... ABOUT CERTAIN THINGS

First of all, let's make one thing abundantly clear...

Medicare is a wonderful healthcare system that helps millions of Americans. Without Medicare, many people would not be able to afford the care that they need when they need it.

For most people, Medicare is guaranteed, because they worked and paid into the system. (Even for those who didn't, there are still government assistance programs available). Overall, we are fans of Medicare.

However, nothing is perfect.

While Medicare covers quite a few things, it doesn't cover everything. We'll make an easy, side-by-side comparison for you shortly. The healthcare system can be considered equally as complicated. There are so many "what ifs?" and exclusions. Folks are surprised to learn some of the things Medicare does *not* cover. That's one of the main points of this book. We will examine what Medicare does *not* cover with respect to long-term care and educate everyone – financial professionals and consumers alike – about the different ways to fill in those coverage gaps to create a comprehensive plan. We are here to debunk some common myths and misconceptions surrounding Medicare. Besides long-term care, there are many other healthcare-related items for which Medicare either provides limited benefits or simply does not cover at all. Some of these include but are not limited to: hearing, dental, vision, certain cancer treatments, and other experimental treatments.

There are certain Medicare supplements you can purchase alongside original Medicare and certain Medicare Advantage plans can help cover some of the gaps of original Medicare. Generally, you will need to buy supplemental insurance such as a dental plan, short-term home healthcare plan, cancer policy, long-term care policy, etc. to ensure that you're wholly covered.

Now you can start to see how the premium for healthcare coverage even on Medicare can add up quickly in order to have comprehensive coverage. We will touch lightly on some of the things that Medicare does not cover besides long-term care, but again, the main focus of this book is long-term care and long-term care insurance. It is the most misunderstood and most commonly needed coverage because it affects so many people. It can be life-changing both emotionally and financially. Even if you don't have a dental plan and you need to get a cavity filled, it's not that big of a deal. However, if you get diagnosed with a chronic illness and there's no coverage in place, you could run through your life savings and put your family through a significant emotional burden.

In summary, here are a few items to note where Medicare is either limited, or doesn't cover at all.
(1) Medicare doesn't cover custodial care long-term care (also known as personal care or intermediate care)

(2) Hearing, dental, vision (some Medicare Advantage plans have this)
(3) Certain cancer treatments
(4) Certain experimental medical treatments
(5) Certain prescription drugs
(6) Co-pays and deductibles
(7) Note: **Medicare is not free**

Let's look at the basics of Medicare:

Medicare Part A, which deals with hospital care, is free, provided that you've adequately paid into the system and met certain guidelines. Medicare Part B, which deals with medical insurance, comes with a monthly premium. If you add a Medicare supplement, that also has an additional premium and so would any additional coverages like hearing, dental, or vision. Some Medicare Advantage plans cover all of this at little to no "cost," but the coverages, themselves, can be extremely limited. Be sure to have a true side-by-side comparison of original Medicare/supplement and Medicare Advantage – both can be good for the right person and the right circumstances.

Frequently, we hear clients saying that they "don't need long-term care insurance, because they have Medicare, and it's free." This is where the education phase begins. There are very few things that are "free." You will need to keep in mind your deductible and copay. Depending on the plan and type of Medicare options you choose, i.e. original Medicare or Medicare Advantage, the co-pays and deductibles vary. We won't focus on these specifics, since this book's educational focus is on long-term care, but please keep these factors in mind when working with your Medicare agent and be sure to have a clear understanding to limit any surprises.

Most of the marketing and sales aspect of Medicare is oriented around what *IS* covered – the bells and whistles of the plan. We have found over the years that very little is typically discussed about what is *NOT* covered. So, we simply want to provide financial professionals and consumers with the knowledge to protect themselves and their loved ones through informed decisions. If you understand what Medicare does *NOT* cover, only then can you plan for the future in a meaningful way.

In fact, most of what Medicare doesn't cover are the very ailments that affect most Americans. As folks age, they are likely to need hearing, dental, and vision services. These are not covered by Medicare. And there is a 50 to 70 percent likelihood that those over the age of 65 will need some sort of long-term care. This is not covered by Medicare, yet most Americans have little to no long-term care insurance. We will insure our cell phones and gadgets before considering long-term care…until now. Imagine, if there was a 70 percent chance that your home would need to be rebuilt at some point. *Wouldn't you have the most coverage possible?* To help you understand a bit more about the relevant statistics, here are few interesting facts:

During your lifetime there is a:
- 25 percent chance that you will have a reported fire in your home (not burned down, just reported)*
- 26 percent chance of an auto injury*
- 70 percent chance of needing some level of long-term care assistance*
    So, why wouldn't you want some level of protection? You can

always buy another house or car, but once you need long-term care, it's too late for any type of significant coverage options.

Let's take a look at how Medicare will cover some areas of long-term care insurance. Keep in mind in order for Medicare to pay for coverage, specific circumstances must be met and will only fully cover skilled nursing (SN) for a limited time. Medicare is federal health insurance that provides only limited coverage for long-term care services. Here is a high-level breakdown:

(1) Will only cover skilled nursing (not personal or custodial care).
(2) Pays the full cost up to 20 days only after three full days of hospitalization.
(3) Pays partial cost from days 21-100 (patient pays $200 coinsurance per day in 2023).
(4) From days 101 onward, it pays NOTHING.
(5) Home health benefits are extremely limited.

Not everyone will qualify for these benefits. Here's how the qualification process works: (this is just a summary, and other factors are involved, but it will give you the general idea).

(1) Your doctor prescribes the skilled nursing care.
(2) You need skilled nursing care every day, not just five or six days a week (unless it's for rehabilitation services only— then, you must get therapy every day services are offered).
(3) You were in the hospital for at least three consecutive days before entering the skilled nursing facility.

Let's take a deep dive into number (3):

Getting to the third-day hospitalization requirement may pose issues, since your doctor may order observation services to help decide whether you need to be admitted to the hospital as an inpatient or can be discharged. During the time you're receiving observation services in the hospital, you're considered an <u>outpatient</u>—you cannot count this time towards the three-day <u>inpatient</u> hospital stay needed for Medicare to cover your skilled nursing facility.

You can see that it may require up to five days at minimum in the hospital. For example, one day inpatient, three days as a patient, and one day for discharge. This is where the lines can blur. The discharge date doesn't generally count toward your three-day required minimum stay by Medicare standards. Be sure that you fully understand this in the event a family member needs to go to a skilled nursing facility. You may be able to work with the provider in this situation.

Once approved, there are some additional requirements:

You must receive skilled nursing care within 30 days after your hospital stay for the same health condition.

Your skilled nursing facility must:
- Participate in the Medicare program.
- Agree with your doctor that you need the care.
- Provide the required level of skilled nursing care.
- Provide skilled rehabilitation services.

<u>Considering these limitations, Medicare only covers roughly 13 percent of long-term care expenses!</u>

<u>In fact, about 95 percent of care is actually classified as custodial care.</u>

What about home healthcare? Won't Medicare cover this?

Yes and no. Here are some of the guidelines to keep in mind for home care:

(1) You need at least part-time skilled nursing care or physical/speech therapy.
(2) Your doctor must prescribe home healthcare and set you up on a home health program.
(3) Your home health providers (the folks that come to the house) must be approved by Medicare. You cannot have family members come take care of you unless they work for a Medicare-approved provider.
(4) Home confinement: If you are confined at home, Medicare will step in. Again, the days are limited as referenced above and in order to be confined at home means:

You have trouble leaving your home without help (like using a cane, wheelchair, walker, crutches, special transportation, or help from another person).

Due to illness or injury, leaving your home isn't recommended, and you're normally unable to leave your home because it's a major effort.

You may leave home for medical treatment or short, infrequent absences for non-medical reasons, like attending religious services. You can still get home healthcare if you attend <u>adult daycare.</u>

We have a breakdown of all the common terminology and definitions in the back of the book. Please feel free to reference this as you proceed.

Can you foresee any challenges or difficulties? Hence why having a plan in place is important and why having back-up and additional insurance coverages to fill these voids can help!

We will explore options to fill the gaps in coverage for custodial care, also known as extended care or long-term care. Some options are certainly better than others. Each option has its own unique place and just as no two people are exactly alike, no two long-term care solutions are exactly alike either.

Some folks won't qualify for certain plans. These plans are not guaranteed – a consumer can be declined. For some, health concerns present eligibility issues, while others have financial limitations. Fortunately, there can be a solution for *everyone*. Read on to learn how you can help yourself and others plan for what might be the hardest time in your lives, their lives, and the lives of their families.

If you or someone you know has personally lived through a long-term care situation, you understand how difficult it is for everyone involved. Without adequate planning, the situation can seem hopeless and near-impossible.

Food for thought:

If you asked someone going through a long-term care event if they could go back in time and buy long-term care insurance (LTCi) would they? The answer is a resounding "yes!" Not enough folks are talking about it. Some folks don't purchase LTCi simply because they don't know about it or they have an archaic preconceived notion about long-term care insurance. ***Are you going to be asking yourself that same question?***

CHAPTER 2

LONG-TERM CARE OVERVIEW

Long-term care – also known as extended care – relates to the assistance needed for mental and/or physical impairments. If you are unable to perform two out of the six daily living activities and/or have a cognitive impairment, you may qualify for needing extended care. Long-term care (LTC) starkly contrasts with *acute* impairments, as we will see. In fact, when most of us think about medical treatment, we are thinking of the treatment of acute symptoms. When you break your leg or have a heart attack, for example, you have an acute condition.

But what if you can't bathe or dress yourself? What if you have memory trouble that limits your ability to respond to everyday situations? What if your recovery is expected to last months or years? And most importantly, what if you develop a condition from which you will *never* recover, but you require assistance to manage the condition?

These are the types of questions addressed by long-term care planning.

There are a multitude of options available in today's marketplace. This book will highlight the major categories of LTC insurance and help you navigate through the sea of choices with which you are faced. Keep in mind, a long-term care event doesn't just happen to really old people; there are strong statistical numbers showing folks receiving care under the age of 70. The average claiming age bracket is between 80-90, but you just never know.

We don't want this book to be "stats heavy," but there are a few important numbers to keep in mind as we move forward and many of these figures will be repeated throughout the reading. We will give you the highlight reel and press ahead:

Who needs care?:

According to the U.S. Department of Health and Human Services, **70 percent of people over age 65** will need some form of long-term care.

Source: U.S. Department of Health and Human Services, October 10, 2017

Note: We share this stat since it is commonly referred to by insurance companies and advisors alike, however, these stats and many others are created using different data points. Some are agreeable by professionals in the LTC space and others not so much. The reality is that you may never need long-term care, and even if there was only a "40 percent" chance of needing it, would you not still plan accordingly? Don't buy LTCi because of statistics— get it because you care about your family.

Let's put this into perspective:

Based on U.S. Census data, there are more than 40 million Americans over the age of 65. That means that there could be 28 million American men and women who may require some level of long-term care (*National Nursing Home Survey*, 2015).

Of those, roughly 12.6 million said that they not only had chronic conditions, but that these chronic conditions were *limiting* American men and women who may require some level of long-term care (*National Nursing Home Survey*, 2015). And these are just the folks who reported that! What about all those who weren't counted or refused to admit that they needed help? How many people do *you* know who say they're fine when they could really use assistance?

About 1.6 million of these elderly persons are permanently confined to a nursing home—American men and women who may require some level of long-term care (*National Nursing Home Survey*, 2015). The rest might require assistance in other facilities or have the need for *in-home assistance*. Most folks associate long-term care with nursing homes, but this is not always true.

Over half of the folks who receive LTC (58 percent) live in their own home. And about 20 percent live in the home of their primary caregiver (Whiting et al., 2020)

<u>Only a fraction of all long-term care occurs in a nursing home or similar facility.</u>

Finally, as we move forward, it will be important to keep in mind that the average length of a long-term care claim is about three years, and women typically need care for longer than men (*How Much Care Will You Need? | ACL Administration for Community Living*, n.d.).

But, when we factor in cognitive impairments and medical advances, the **average length of claim** climbs to **five years**! As we will see, there are no other types of coverage that will take care of someone in a chronic care situation other than chronic/long-term care, itself. As medical technology advances and people are living longer, people are staying on claim much longer as well. 15 to 20 years from now, who knows what the average stay of claim will be! Will it be 8 to 10 years or longer? This is where we help people become educated and understand that having a plan for long-term care should incorporate the potential need for coverage for a long period of time.

If you search the Internet, you can easily find information about the average age folks go on claim and the average claim duration. The majority of these stats are generated from Medicaid, which means that a lot of these people have already gone through their assets, savings, investments, other retirement plans, rental properties, etc. to pay for care. Only then will they potentially qualify for Medicaid, the free state/federal program.

What a lot of people don't realize is that after an individual passes away, the states are required to go back and audit their estate to ensure that they did, indeed, qualify for Medicaid. If the audit finds that you did not qualify, then they have the right to go after the remaining assets to pay the bill! It can turn into a very lengthy and complicated process with everybody's best friends being involved…the attorneys!

Why in the world would anyone want to put their family through this? Most folks aren't even aware of this or how the Medicaid program works.

The Medicaid program is state-specific. It's always important to speak with your agent/estate planning attorney or do your own research on your residence state's requirements for Medicaid eligibility. We are not going to get into the weeds with Medicaid. Rather, we will show you ways to prevent a Medicaid situation if possible. Ultimately, people want the choice of where they want care. Do you really want to rely on your state to take care of you? Tell you where to go? Provide you with services that they feel are applicable to you? Wouldn't it be much better to have your own choices or to have your family make choices for you with adequate financial means to do so?

A Family Affair:

Most folks don't consider long-term care unless they live alone or don't have family to take care of them. But it's just as important to have a plan when you *do* have family in the picture.

Think about elderly spouses taking care of each other. What if one of them falls? Can the other lift them? What if one of them needs help bathing or toileting? Is the other strong enough to provide the necessary support?

Stress-related illnesses and death in elderly caregivers becomes 63 percent more likely (Schulz et al., 2013)!

Okay, now let's suppose the person in need of care has adult children who are able to take care of them. First of all, does the care recipient want to be a burden on their children? And what type of sacrifices must a family member make when providing care? In some situations, providing care for a family member becomes a full-time job!

Let's look at some of the numbers relating to family members as caregivers:

Over 34 million Americans have been care providers for a family member over the age of 50, and over 15 million of those folks have provided care for someone with Alzheimer's or dementia (*2015 Alzheimer's Disease Facts and Figures*, 2015)!

Of these caregivers, 69 percent have said they needed to modify their work schedules or take unpaid leave. Some caregivers reported elevated stress and anxiety, and about 22 percent even reported depression (Schulz et al., 2013).

Caregivers of family members have stated that their health has decreased as a direct result of their providing care. They mentioned a variety of health concerns like weight loss/gain (38 percent) or loss of sleep/energy (87 percent). 69 percent noted that they spend less time with friends (Evercare & National Alliance for Caregiving, 2006).

It's comforting to know that we have family willing to take care of us in our time of need. But we need to stop and consider the ramifications that our care will have on our loved ones.

We haven't even gotten to the financial aspect yet, and already we must ask ourselves,

"What is the real cost of care?"

We said from the beginning that we didn't want to be too "stats" heavy, but it's important to keep these elements in mind as we move forward.

The real cost of care, as we've determined, is the hardship it can place on our loved ones. But just so we're clear, it can also be financially expensive. In 2019, the average cost of nursing home care nationally was **$89,297 per year.** And that's an average! That means depending on where you live, the cost can be much higher (Seniorliving.org, 2023).

Most people who need care simply cannot afford it!

Therefore, they will rely on family members, and we've already seen the negative impact this causes.

So, what's the answer?

What do you think the cost will be in the future? If 70 percent of people are likely to need some level of long-term care in the largest generation ever created in the history of the world (the Baby Boomers, with close to 10,000 per day turning 65), can you see a supply-and-demand situation? Additionally, you must consider inflationary pressures. Simply put, the cost of goods and services increase over time. How much was a new car 30 years ago? A lot less than it is today!

When it comes to long-term care planning, we definitely want to consider what the cost could be in the future. The long-term care plan, itself, may not cover everything, but <u>something is better than nothing</u>, and it will at least help create additional cash flow on a tax-advantaged basis. You must think of long-term care as a selfless product and strategy. It *is* for you, but really, it's for your family.

Long-Term Care Insurance

LTC insurance options are designed to ensure your family (spouse/children/etc.) can maintain their lifestyle and standard of living while you get the care you need.

LTC insurance options keep you in the driver's seat of your care—you choose where and how you can receive care. We get it: nobody wants to buy insurance — especially long-term care insurance. It's something that nobody even wants to talk about. Who wants to talk about the possibility of having their diapers changed by their spouse or children?! But this "bill" or asset reallocation for LTCi may be your saving grace that protects everything you have worked for your whole life.

Most advisors and agents would much rather talk about all the bells and whistles of retirement plans and how they're going to live this happy retirement dream, sailing the world, etc. But if this is not the case, how do we protect your legacy, your estate, and your family's emotional and physical well-being? These are hard conversations that are often overlooked or not emphasized enough during a financial planning, insurance meeting, or estate planning setting.

CHAPTER 3

UNDERSTANDING THE WHY

No one needs long-term care insurance (LTCi)….<u>until they do</u>. We've already demonstrated the huge toll that providing care creates on our loved ones. Yet, there will always be folks who claim that they don't need LTCi.

The two most common objections that we've found are:
1) "I won't get sick, and I won't need care." and
2) "I can find a different and better source to fund my care if I need it."

By the time you've finished this book, you can easily handle these common objections. We will touch a bit on these now as we explore how to educate ourselves on the need for LTCi. We will cover these objections in-depth a bit later in the self-funding chapter. But for now, let's focus conceptually on "the why."

The longer we live, the higher the likelihood that we will need care…and people are living much longer these days! By logical extension, that means that folks are living longer <u>with their ailments</u>! Medical advancements 15 to 20 years in the future might even increase this timeline!

Let's look at some different financial/net worth classes and examine some of the care options. We'll also consider some of the objections you may be having and questions you may be asking.

We'll ask some questions of our own, so you can think through them to figure out what's best for you.

Let's look at a couple scenarios:
   A)   <u>You or your loved one has a low income/net worth</u>:

        If they need care, they will likely find themselves needing the help of Medicaid. We will see in a later chapter why this can be problematic. However, if financial resources are limited, at least there are programs available to provide assistance.

   B)   <u>You or your loved one has a middle income/net worth</u>:

        If they need care, they might have the assets to pay for the care at first, but as we will see, these assets can deplete quickly, and we can still find ourselves in a Medicaid situation. Or, what if one spouse uses up all the assets for his/her care and the surviving spouse enters into a care event...but all the assets are gone?!

        The last thing you or anyone wants to do is give away everything for which they've worked so hard – especially when we can potentially avoid this and at least limit the liquidation and taxation of your life's savings/assets.

   C)   <u>You or your loved one has a high income/net worth</u>:

        We've already seen the cost of care both emotionally and financially. A care event can even drain down the assets of the affluent. It can have a negative impact on the legacy these individuals are able to leave behind. But a serious question to ask someone or yourself if you are high net worth is this:

"Even if you *can* afford to pay for your own care, why would you want to?!"

LTCi provides options, as we will see, to leverage funds and create two, three, five, or even ten times the amount of money you put in. Another way of looking at this is you can spend "other people's money" (a.k.a. the insurance company's money) on your own care.

Ask yourself the following questions:

If your house is paid off, would you still carry homeowner's insurance?"

Do you think there's a higher likelihood that your house will burn down or that you'll get sick in the future and need assistance?

If you are going to self-insure then why buy Medicare or health insurance at all?

Hopefully it is starting to click!

CHAPTER 4

LTCi OPTIONS

There is a long-term care option for everyone – even if it's Medicaid.

Medicaid most certainly does *not* have the nicest or most robust coverage options, but something is better than nothing. There are other countries that have *nothing*, and it's 100 percent up to the family to provide care.

Long-term care plans vary, and some will offer more benefits than others, but there is something for everyone. There is the "sports car" option and the "daily commuter" option. Even for folks who don't have the extra income or the assets to reallocate, they can still write out a plan and have some level of coverage.

There are options for folks of every income bracket, social status, age, or any other characteristic we can use to define a category.

Since everyone's means and needs are different, every plan will be different. A good agent will ask the right questions and custom fit options that fill their clients' needs.

Everyone is unique. Every plan is unique.

There's a difference between a good plan and a poor plan. When you start to consider long-term care insurance, you need to work with someone who is experienced. There are a lot of people in the industry who have the ability to write long-term care insurance, but do they specialize in it? When you're looking for long-term care options, you should ask your agent how many companies they work with, how long have they been doing it, and what plan they have for themselves or what plan have they utilized to help their own family members?

Below is a short list of some things to consider that a good agent should be providing.

A good agent will consider features like:
- The health of the insured
- The benefits available
- The benefit triggers
- The elimination (or waiting) period before benefits begin
- The location of care
- The cost of the plan
- How the benefits are paid out (indemnity or reimbursement)
- Full financial fact finder and financial goals
- Inflation protection

Finding the right long-term care insurance plan is all about education. We believe fully in educating our clients regarding their options and then letting them choose what suits them. Of course, as specialists, we will provide the pros and cons of each option, but ultimately, the choice is yours.

The next part of the book will take us through the different extended care planning options in individual detail.

From a high level, the options are:

- Medicaid
- Medicare
- Short-term care
- Home healthcare
- Nursing home care
- "Traditional" long-term care
- Asset-based care
- Life insurance hybrids
- Annuity options
- Self-funding

Now, let's explore the options…

CHAPTER 5

MEDICAID

Medicaid is a federal/state program that helps pay for long-term care expenses. In fact, it is the largest public payer. It sounds great, right? The government will take care of you if you develop a chronic illness or need care!

If it sounds too good to be true...

In order to qualify for Medicaid, you must meet certain state and federal requirements based on your income and assets. These requirements are fairly strict and limit most individuals who have retirement assets/retirement income to qualify. These requirements vary per state, but essentially, they will only cover those who have very little income in retirement. Even if you qualify, your choices are limited and restricted to facilities that are approved by the Medicaid program. In other words, you must be poor, or deplete your hard-earned assets and *become* poor. Medicaid eligibility will look at all sources of income, cash, insurance, investments, and financial assets to determine if you qualify. Keep in mind, qualifying does not happen overnight and may take months. What would you do in the meantime? Another important thing to consider is that your options are limited where you receive care. If you'd prefer to remain at home instead of a facility, this may not happen. This could cause you to lose your independence and be forced into a sub-par facility.

I know what you're thinking…I'll just gift away my assets to my heirs until I qualify!

Medicaid has "look back" periods of up to five years and complicated ineligibility guidelines. In short, Medicaid is there to help those who are unable to afford care on their own. It's great if you have nothing else. It is a safety net that exists to take care of those who cannot take care of themselves. This is surface level, it gets way more complicated with details, if you feel you may qualify for Medicaid, do your research and read up on it.

Also, to address another common question we get asked about Medicaid: Yes, there are ways to create trusts that reposition assets that Medicaid does not "count" towards qualification. Be careful of these types of planning situations and *really* understand what is going on.

NB: EACH STATE IS DIFFERENT, AND THE MEDICAID RULES ARE ALWAYS CHANGING.

A good relationship with an attorney is crucial. Always stay current with your state's specific guidelines.

CHAPTER 6

MEDICARE

Medicare is *not* a strategy for extended care. It only covers *skilled* and *rehabilitative* care. Medicare is designed to treat and release. But what about those who have a need for prolonged care? What about those with a chronic illness or cognitive impairment? Medicare is a useful and essential part of our healthcare system – it's just not designed for extended care.

When talking to your clients about Medicare, you need to know what services and procedures Medicare covers. But, from an extended care perspective, let's look at what Medicare **does not** cover.

Medicare only covers the first 100 days in a skilled nursing facility. After that, it covers…***nothing***! Can you be sure that you will not need care beyond 100 days? **No!**

And, to make matters worse, Medicare will only cover the *full* cost of a skilled nursing facility for 20 days – Days 21-100 are not fully covered. As mentioned earlier, there is a co-pay for these days. As of 2023, it's $200 per day that *you* must pay, then they pay the difference. On day 101, it's all on you.

Here's a quick breakdown of Medicare 2023. These figures change every year! So, stay informed and updated, so you know your cost and coverages. You have the option to buy a supplement to cover the additional cost not covered by Medicare, or you can have a Medicare Advantage plan. Just be careful, as these plans are often marketed as "free" or "low cost" but there are significant differences and drawbacks including MOOP's (maximum out of pocket), which can total in the tens of thousands of dollars.

Medicare Part A (hospital insurance) costs for 2023
- Part A deductible for inpatient hospitalization: $1,600 per benefit period (up from $1,556 in 2022).
- Part A premium for those who need to buy coverage: up to $506 per month (up from $499 in 2022) — most people don't pay a premium for Medicare Part A.
- Part A coinsurance: $400 per day for days 61 through 90, and $800 per "lifetime reserve day" after day 90, up to a 60-day lifetime maximum (up from $389 and $778 in 2022).
- Part A skilled nursing facility coinsurance: $200 for days 21 through 100 for each benefit period (up from $194.50 in 2022).

Medicare Part B (medical insurance) costs for 2023

Most people with Medicare who receive Social Security benefits will pay the standard monthly Part B premium of $164.90 in 2023. This premium is $5.20 lower than it was in 2022 due to lower-than-projected spending for a new drug, Aduhelm, and other Part B items and services.

People with higher incomes may pay more than the standard premium. If your modified adjusted gross income (MAGI) as reported on your federal income tax return from two years ago (2021) is above a certain amount, you'll pay the standard premium amount and an income-related monthly adjustment amount (IRMAA), which is an extra charge added to your premium, as shown in the following table.

You filed an individual income tax return with MAGI that was:	You filed a joint income tax return with MAGI that was:	You filed an income tax return as married filing separately with MAGI that was:	Total monthly premium in 2023 is:	*Total monthly premium in 2023 immunosuppressive drug coverage only is:
$97,000 or less	$194,000 or less	$97,000 or less	$164.90	$97.10
Above $97,000 up to $123,000	Above $194,000 up to $246,000	N/A	$230.80	$161.80
Above $123,000 up to $153,000	Above $246,000 up to $306,000	N/A	$329.70	$258.90
Above $153,000 up to $183,000	Above $306,000 up to $366,000	N/A	$428.60	$356.00
Above $183,000 and less than $500,000	Above $366,000 and less than $750,000	Above $97,000 and less than $403,000	$527.50	$453.10
$500,000 and above	$750,000 and above	$403,000 and above	$560.50	$485.50

People with higher incomes may also pay a higher premium for a Medicare Part D prescription drug plan, because an IRMAA will be added to the Part D basic premium based on the same income limits in the table above. Part D premiums vary, but the average basic monthly premium for 2023 is projected to be $31.50 (down from $32.08 in 2022).

People with Medicare Part B must also satisfy an annual deductible before original Medicare starts to pay. For 2023, this deductible is $226 (down from $233 in 2022).

Now, let's look at some of the ways we can fill in the gaps.

CHAPTER 7

SHORT-TERM PLANS - HOME HEALTHCARE/NURSING HOME

Short-term plans can be amazingly beneficial programs for decreasing risk under certain circumstances. Let's keep in mind that these plans will only cover 360 days in most situations. The qualifications to activate the policy and receive claim money is generally the same as it is for a traditional long-term care policy.

For example, short-term (nursing home) policies can:
- Offset the elimination periods in some more traditional plans.
- Provide "day one" benefit coverage, which is helpful if you do not qualify under Medicare's definitions or your nursing home is not considered skilled care.
- Protect a policyholder from having to take a withdrawal or loan against a policy or financial account for a short-term stay.
- Provide a lower cost alternative, that while not as comprehensive as other options, may be much more affordable.
- Give the client time and resources to make any substantial changes that they may have to make.
- Typically, when asked where they would like to receive care, folks will select an option for *at home care*. Home healthcare-specific plans can be used to:

- Provide at-home alternatives for different levels of care.
- Offset the potential halving of the primary benefit in some LTC policies in case of use for home healthcare.
- Provide a lower cost alternative that while not as comprehensive as other options may be much more affordable and address the primary concerns of the consumer.
- These plans are also generally less stringent on underwriting, so for older people (75+) or those with health issues, a short-term plan may be ideal.

Generally, it is best to purchase a short-term home healthcare plan AND a short-term nursing home policy. When policies are purchased for specific coverages, you often get a better benefit.

In all, both short-term nursing home and home healthcare coverage can be valuable options for a consumer, depending on their situation, needs, and primary concerns. Even for very affluent people, we still recommend short-term plans. They provide additional benefits, gap coverage to pay out during elimination periods, and ultimately, additional funding. Who knows what the cost of care is going to be when you need it? Most of these policies can be purchased for less than $100 a month for a basic level of coverage!

CHAPTER 8

LONG-TERM CARE INSURANCE PAYOUT OPTIONS

Long-term care insurance is actually a two-part application. The first part is to see if you even qualify for the coverage. This means that the insurance company must be willing to offer you the coverage.

<u>Everyone can have some level of long-term care insurance</u>. There are *guaranteed* options and other ways to position assets to create leverage and help pay for a long-term care situation. The better plans, however, do require a relatively healthy background.

This is the first part — being accepted.

The second part is getting the money from the insurance company if you go onto claim. Fortunately, the claims process has improved over the last decade, making it easier for people to receive the money from the insurance company to help pay for the facility or the in-home services. There are two types of benefits that you can receive from your long-term care insurance contract — **reimbursement and indemnity**.

A **reimbursement** plan means that the insurance company will pay for qualified long-term care expenses *only*. These services can be rendered at home or at a facility. There is nothing wrong with this type of coverage, and it is the original payout method for long-term care insurance. You could also see it as a protection barrier, because the money cannot be spent frivolously by family members; it can only be used for qualified care. However, there are restrictions and limitations. Qualified long-term care services are generally more expensive, and the options can be limited.

The other type of payout factor is **indemnity**. An indemnity plan means that the insurance company will literally pay out the money to your personal checking account, and you can spend it however you choose. Of course, you must *qualify* for care with a doctor certification, but once those are met, you can literally spend the money in Las Vegas with your family. You probably won't be in the situation to enjoy it, but this is just to demonstrate that there are no restrictions on how the money can be spent.

The value here is that you have total control over the way you receive your care. Perhaps you want to pay a family member to come take care of you and that family member is not certified. With this type of policy, you can do that! Perhaps you want to use the money to fly in family from all over the country to come visit you. You can do that with this type of policy!

Like anything else in life, there's always a give and take. The more flexibility you have, the less leverage you'll get from the insurance company. Health requirements for indemnity plans tend to be a little stricter.

In simple terms, having an indemnity policy is great, and in our opinion, if we had an unlimited checkbook, it's the way to go! However, indemnity plans are more expensive dollar-for-dollar. For instance, a married couple can purchase one reimbursement policy to cover them both, with benefits lasting for life with very good coverage rates. If the same couple wanted to have total freedom of how the money is spent, they would need to go the indemnity route. It may require twice the premium to have equal benefits. Some folks just don't have that type of discretionary income/assets to justify the expense.

The point is this: when working with a good agent, you should explore both options.

CHAPTER 9

TRADITIONAL LTC

Traditional LTC policies are designed for long-term care and nothing else. Well, our job here is done!

Unfortunately, it's not quite that simple.

With a traditional LTC policy, the insurance carrier agrees to pay a specified benefit amount in exchange for a monthly or annual premium. The contract states the qualifications a person must meet in order to go on claim.

When the insured meets these requirements, the insurance company pays from a predetermined "pool" of money. When that money is exhausted, so is the contract. Some of the older contracts had lifetime benefits. In today's marketplace, it's virtually impossible to find that with a traditional LTC policy. There are some, but the payment options into them are limited. To get these types of benefits, you usually need to go with a hybrid policy. You also want to look at how long the benefit period is and if it's based on a shared pool of money (benefits) i.e a joint policy between husband and wife or if it's based on an individual pool of money, i.e single owned policy or separate benefits. The average is about a three year benefit period.

We generally aim to help folks with at least six years of coverage. This is a longer-than-average stay on claim. However, there are cases where people have been on claim 8, 10, 15, and even 20+ years!

There are only 100 pennies in a dollar, so it's important to maximize coverage, balanced with your budget. This is where working with a professional is important, so that way you can evaluate all the options and get a true side-by-side comparison.

But there are some drawbacks:

If you never need to go on claim and you pass away, the policy passes with you. Some policies may offer a small premium refund, but they don't have a robust death benefit or cash balance you pass on to your heirs. They are simply not designed that way. If you are married and own a joint policy, you may be able to inherit your deceased spouse's benefits. This depends on the contract. Long-term care insurance policies can have dozens of variations and differences. This is why we offer complimentary reviews for our clients. When looking for a good agent/advisor, be sure they offer free reviews on pre-existing policies.

Traditional long-term care policies can offer great leverage and very affordable coverage, but there are some potential risks associated with these types of policies, such as premium increase. Some of the older policies had premium rate guarantees, and there are still options today for this, but the premium dramatically increases and may become unaffordable for most.

Rate Increases:

The insurance carriers may reserve the right to raise premiums on blocks of business sold during a specific timeframe. There have been rate increases of more than 600 percent! Imagine that you pay your bill on time every month and you do everything you're supposed to do, and then, in 20 years, the insurance company raises rates, and the policy becomes unaffordable. What then?

Well, you have some settlement options. Instead of a rate increase, the company might offer to reduce the benefit amount. In either case, the consumer must give something up.

> ***Please note**: These rate increases happen less frequently in today's marketplace than they have historically. Products are much better priced to ensure that rates will not have to rise as often in the future. However, sometimes this means the initial price is higher as well. While rate increases are not likely, they still can happen.

Tax and Medicaid Benefits with Traditional Long-Term Care Policies:

Traditional long-term care insurance policies can have unique tax and state partnership programs. The state partnership programs vary from state to state, just like the Medicaid rules do. However, one simple explanation of how the state partnership policies can add value is by helping with the Medicaid asset exclusion calculations (asset disregard) . For instance, let's assume you had a traditional long-term care policy that was a part of the state partnership program which paid out a total benefit of $350,000. When you go to apply for Medicaid, $350,000 will be subtracted from your total asset calculation, potentially allowing you to qualify for Medicaid more easily. As previously mentioned, Medicaid planning can be tricky. Even if you qualify, the state that you reside in will most likely look back at your estate after you pass to ensure that you did, indeed, qualify. Currently, there is a five-year look-back period. If your state discovers that you had more assets than what meets their guidelines, they can go after your estate to get that money back that was spent on you while on Medicaid. This is why there are law firms that specialize in elderly care and Medicaid planning, the system can be complex.

If you own or plan to own any type of long-term care insurance, it is important to know the various nuances and tax advantages. In fact, there's also federal and state income tax deduction opportunities for traditional long-term care policies. These tax deductions can also apply to hybrid policies, also known as asset-based long-term care. The main thing to look for is how the policies are classified taxwise. Some policies are a life insurance acceleration and not technically long-term care, which does not offer the same tax deductions as long-term care insurance. At the same note, some of the hybrid policies that are classified as long-term care for tax purposes are not a part of the state partnership program, meaning that there could be no asset disregard when it comes to total benefits paid out on the Medicaid asset calculations. There are other corporate tax deductions beyond individual policies. For instance, businesses can own policies on their key employees and partners and receive tax deductions and tax advantages, but in this book, we're not going to focus on the nitty-gritty details of taxes. You can reach out to our team directly or work with your CPA or tax professional to see how you may be able to benefit.

CHAPTER 10

ASSET BASED LTCI - LIFE INSURANCE AND ANNUITIES

Okay, so now we know a bit more about traditional long-term care insurance, let's take a look at some of the other alternatives and ways to leverage your money with tax efficiency. The most exciting and innovative type of extended care planning is what we call <u>asset-based LTCi</u>.

Asset-based long-term care insurance utilizes different insurance products to leverage money for future care expenses. We can set up monthly/annual payments or earmark assets from an existing portfolio and allocate them for LTC. These options are a separate asset class from traditional investments and have certain tax advantages. (They are insurance products even though they can use retirement money, including IRAs).

Unlike traditional policies, asset-based LTCi policies have unique features like: single premium payments, payments over time, death benefit options, return of premium options, liquidity provisions, life insurance features, and perhaps most importantly, guaranteed contract provisions.

The two main vehicles for Asset Based LTCi are
1) Life insurance

2) Annuities

<u>Remember: the goal of the agent is to help the client understand the benefits and policy details.</u>

<u>Agents are educators.</u> Be sure your agent is an educator — not a used car salesman.

When educated properly, *you* will make this decision, and the agent will simply help you with the paperwork because you cannot purchase this on your own. You will need a licensed professional to work with you. Generally, the insurance companies don't sell long-term care directly to consumers, and even if they did, the person on the other line has an insurance license.

CHAPTER 11

LIFE INSURANCE "HYBRIDS"

COMBINATION PLANS WITH DEATH BENEFIT AND LTC/LIVING BENEFIT OPTIONS

LIFE INSURANCE IS MORE THAN JUST "DEATH INSURANCE"

Contrary to what most people think, life insurance isn't just "if you die, your family gets money." This is an oversimplification. Life insurance comes in all shapes and sizes and employs different strategies depending on the needs of the individual. As we will see, we can use life insurance in clever ways to leverage money for LTC expenses. There are other policies that are life insurance-based, but are not designed to leave a large death benefit—rather, they are designed to provide long-term care. We will go over those in detail after this section.

But first, let's consider some of the benefits of life insurance over and above the death benefit:

The Benefits of Life Insurance

Death benefit:

The primary function of life insurance is the death benefit. This benefit is paid to your listed beneficiaries income *tax free*. That's right!

Your heirs won't have to pay a dime in income taxes from the payable benefit of a life insurance policy. Dollar-for-dollar, there is no other financial strategy that can provide this type of tax-advantaged leverage.

Cash return option:

Some policies have a "cash return" or "return or premium" option. This means that if you ever decide you want to cancel the policy, you get all your money back.

We don't recommend using this option as a _reason_ for buying life insurance. If you think you will cancel the policy, then perhaps a different option is more suitable. However, we also understand that peoples' needs change over time, and it's nice to know this option is there in the event we need it – after all, isn't that the whole point of insurance in the first place?

Guaranteed level premiums:

At the time you sign the contract with the insurance company, you agree to certain monthly/annual premiums. These premiums can be _guaranteed_ never to increase over the life of the contract. Period. (Not all life insurance offers this benefit, so be sure to understand what you are purchasing before singing).

No lump sum required:

Some asset-based LTCi options require large lump sums of cash to start/fund them; life insurance does not. In fact, you can get _day 1 coverage_ in exchange for _fixed_ monthly/annual payments. For example, if you buy a $1,000,000 policy today and are tragically hit by a bus tomorrow, your family will receive $1,000,000.

Most of them will also allow you to pay until you are 100, reducing the monthly cost vs. a 10 pay or lump sum type of policy.

More than a death benefit, many folks today, state dependent, can use their life insurance while they are alive, also known as living benefits. In recent years, life insurance has changed dramatically for the better. In certain circumstances, you can access your death benefit *while you are alive!* You heard that right. In the event of a qualifying illness, a portion of your benefit amount can be advanced to you, so that you can use it while you are still living.

Hence the terminology "living benefit." Often, there is no additional cost associated with these living benefits; they are built right into the policy. You can use the money to offset medical bills, replace lost income from missed work, or any other needs you and your family might have.

With living benefits, life insurance protects not only your family, but it protects *you* as well. It's a win-win.

Let's look at the three most common types of living benefits and the events that might trigger them:

Chronic illness living benefit:

This is commonly defined as a chronic illness that is not recoverable and the individual is unable to perform two out of the six "activities of daily living" **or** has a cognitive impairment such as Alzheimer's or dementia. The 6 "activities of daily living" (or ADL's) are defined as follows:

- Bathing: the ability to clean oneself and perform grooming activities like shaving and brushing teeth.
- Dressing: the ability to get dressed by oneself without struggling with buttons and zippers.
- Eating: the ability to feed oneself.
- Transferring: being able to either walk or move oneself from a bed to a wheelchair and back again.
- Toileting: the ability to get on and off the toilet.
- Continence: the ability to control one's bladder and bowel functions.

Doesn't this sound like the exact situation that would require long-term care insurance?

If you are unable to perform at least two of these six activities, you could qualify to use your life insurance living benefit. Some companies will accelerate a certain percentage of the overall face amount of the policy per year. A monthly 2 percent acceleration equates to up to 24 percent per year, meaning a $1,000,000 policy could yield your family up to $240,000 in the event of a chronic illness. Talk about peace of mind! (The net amount that you receive may differ based on the company's policy and contract terms, but the bottom line is that you will have access to benefits *while you're alive!*)

Are you starting to see how we can use life insurance to create income-tax-free long-term care dollars?! (Also keep in mind that most life insurance accelerated benefits are indemnity-based, meaning you can spend the money however you choose)!

Critical illness living benefit:

What if you're not *chronically* ill, but have a defined *acute* illness?

This does not cover long-term care per se, but oftentimes, we see acute illnesses that lead to chronic conditions. Even if they don't, it's important to understand the critical illness living benefit.

Here is a list of some major acute illnesses:
- Invasive metastatic cancer
- Major burns
- Stroke
- Coma
- Major heart attack
- Aplastic anemia
- End-stage renal failure
- Benign brain tumor
- Major organ transplant
- Aortic aneurysm
- ALS (Amyotrophic Lateral Sclerosis)
- Heart valve replacement
- Blindness due to diabetes
- Coronary artery bypass graft surgery
- Critical illness paralysis of two or more limbs

If one of these situations occurs, you may be entitled to access a portion of your death benefit. Some companies will accelerate your death benefit up to 90 or even 100 percent (the net amount that you receive may differ based on the company's policy and contract terms, but the bottom line is that you will have access to benefits *while you're alive*).

Terminal illness living benefit:

Terminal illness is commonly defined as having less than 12-24 months to live. In this case, you may be able to accelerate up to 90 or even 100 percent of your death benefit. (Like the critical illness and chronic illness living benefits, the net amount you receive may differ based on company policy and contract terms. However, this is a good guideline).

Summary of life insurance benefits:

Life insurance is so much more than people think. If you don't use the benefits for long-term care, your family gets a large **income-tax-free** benefit when you pass away. However, as we've seen, you have several options to use the policy for long-term care *while you're alive*!

There are ways to ensure you get all your money back if you decide to cancel the policy and there are little upfront costs. Plus, if you *do* need to go on a long-term care claim, most companies will waive your monthly premiums as long as the claim is active.

Because of life insurance's unique tax advantages…

All the benefits paid to you for long-term care expenses are 100 percent income-tax-free.

All the benefits paid to your family are 100 percent income-tax-free when you pass away!

Be sure to know how the benefits are paid out (i.e. reimbursement or indemnity).

Finally, if you use *some* of the benefit amount for long-term care expenses and then pass away, <u>your family can receive the remainder of your death benefit!</u> Life insurance allows you to have your cake and eat it too. You win. Your family wins. Everyone wins.

Drawbacks

By now, you're probably thinking that life insurance is too good to be true. (It's not).

You're probably thinking there's no way you can fund your long-term care needs this simply and easily with little to no upfront cash. (You can).

Unfortunately, life insurance isn't all rainbow kisses and unicorn hugs. As with everything, there are some potential drawbacks to consider:

Medical underwriting/qualification:

Most life insurance policies with long-term care benefits are fully medically underwritten. To qualify, insurance companies might ask for an exam, blood/urine, additional health questions, medical records, lifestyle questions, etc.

<u>Life insurance companies reserve the right to refuse service to anyone</u> – not everyone will qualify. However, for those who *can* qualify, this is a great option.

Longer wait times:

Because these policies require more information to see if you're qualified, they take longer to issue than other LTCi options. Some life policies only take a couple of days to become active, but in practice, we've seen policies take several months (and more), depending on the particular case. And there is still no guarantee that you will qualify for coverage.

Having a good agent will mitigate these risks. Good agents will understand certain "knockout questions" for different policies and steer their clients to policies that are a better fit. No one wants to have their time wasted.

Finite benefit amount:

Finally, the LTC benefit amount offered by most life insurance is limited to the face amount of the policy. If you have a $100,000 life insurance policy and you enter into a care event, this will only cover you for a short time. And it might not cover *all* your expenses.

Taking the concept from our earlier example, a $100,000 could provide *up to* $24,000 per year for LTC coverage. As we've seen, $24,000 per year doesn't cover a whole lot of long-term care. There is a risk of running out of money before the need runs out.

But as always…**something is better than nothing!**

Depending on your age, life insurance with an LTC-type benefit may be the most beneficial. Perhaps you have a young family and need life insurance more than LTCi since you are young and have a family to protect. You can combine the two together and get the best of both worlds.

Conclusion

In the wake of COVID, life insurance sales have seen a surge. Folks are starting to come to grips with their own mortality in a very real way. But, more importantly, consumers are seeing the value that life insurance has to offer.

We now know that life insurance is not a "use it or lose it" type of scenario. Life insurance is also for the living!

Life insurance is a clever and cost-effective way to leverage funds for long-term care expenses and can <u>create an income-tax-free income stream to help you and your family when you need it most.</u>

CHAPTER 12

ANNUITY-BASED LTC

What's an annuity?

Annuities have come under fire in recent years and an odd mystique has built up around them. They are commonly misunderstood, probably because there are thousands of variations, options, and most importantly, opinions about annuities.

The word "annuity" comes to us from Old French "annuite" through the Latin, "anuus" for "year." An annuity was simply a payment that occurred on a yearly/monthly basis, and that still holds true today. In fact, the Roman Empire paid their soldiers through an annuity. However, we doubt very seriously that the Romans could have possibly fathomed all the different uses for such a structured payment!

Annuities, for the purpose of our conversation here are going to be long-term care annuities. They are designed to focus on creating leverage for the purpose of paying an enhanced and tax-advantaged benefit. These annuities offer downside protection while allowing the consumer to participate in potential gains. They have no management fees and can be set up with no ongoing policy premiums. In short, they are a *safe money strategy* for long-term care leverage and some growth while providing peace of mind.

Even though long-term care annuities might limit the amount of potential gains compared to other annuities and investment strategies, they provide unparalleled long-term care benefits and unique tax privileges that other annuities simply cannot offer.

Annuities and long-term care:

So, how can we use annuities to cover long-term care expenses?

We have several options:

Annuities for long-term care work best as a single lump sum payment. Some plans can also have monthly/annual premiums associated with them for more robust benefits, but the lump sum buys most of the coverage.

The best candidates for this type of long-term care are those who have an existing portfolio in which they can reallocate some assets. Oftentimes, there is no cost to transfer the assets. The tax code also allows us to move money "like-to-like" without any tax consequences. It will cost the client nothing out of pocket. We like to call this "left pocket to right pocket." We are merely earmarking a portion of the portfolio for long-term care. You must think of the "lump-sum" as a way to instantly provide leverage within the portfolio. The lump sum being parked with the insurance company will be paid back to you when you need care. Then, the insurance company will pay out of their pocket the remaining promised claim amount.

Another way to think about this is "portfolio insurance."

Nearly nothing will deplete a portfolio faster than long-term care expenses. Why in the world would you not want to mitigate some of those risks?!

Long-term care insurance creates tax-free leverage on the existing portfolio and helps provide cash when it's needed most.

Let's look at an example:

Let's say Jim and Lisa have a total retirement portfolio of $1,000,000. They have earmarked $200,000 for potential long-term care expenses…but they don't have long-term care insurance.

If either one of them needs care, they will have to pay for it out-of-pocket, dollar-for-dollar. And, as we've seen, $200,000 doesn't go very far. It might seem like a lot of money, but what if *both* spouses become ill in their lifetimes? One spouse could drain the whole $200,000, and then, they would be drawing from their other assets.

> **<u>Here's an important note</u>**: *A healthy retirement portfolio is not a question of* **assets** *– it's a question of* **income**. *This is one of the most important concepts to understand.*

If you are drawing down on assets, what do you think will happen to the income that's generated from those assets? And what happens if you are forced to draw from the assets in a down market?

You've got it right –income decreases and the risk of outliving your money quickly becomes a potential reality.

Let's not forget about the "sequence of returns rate risk" or "withdrawal rate risk." This comes into play when you are drawing on a portfolio that is depleting due to market corrections or substantial withdrawals. If your million-dollar portfolio is down by 20 percent and you still need to take out 50,000, that is no longer five percent of 1 million — it is a significantly higher percentage, because you have to get 50,000 from 800,000 since it's down by 20 percent.

This is the type of scenario we ask folks to consider with their advisor. Have them run a scenario showing this situation. Additionally, have them run this scenario with an inflation rate of three to five percent. This will help give you a better idea of worst-case scenarios.

In this very same example, how far do you think 50,000 would go to pay for long-term care? Maybe six months? Perhaps a year, depending on the severity of your care?

You can see how the numbers can be daunting.

When was the last time you reviewed this information?

Remember:

Income is what allows you and your spouse to maintain a certain lifestyle and style of living. *Income* is what banks look at if you want a loan.

Income is the most important part of a retirement plan, and assets are simply a way to generate that income.

Long-term care insurance protects both assets and income!

It protects your assets, by limiting the amount you would have to sell off in a long-term care event.

It protects your income because it generates leverage on your existing funds and pays out a daily or monthly tax-free benefit to pay for your care.

How does it work?

Insurance companies issue a contract that explicitly states how the benefits will pay out and how much they will pay. Most companies offer at least a 3:1 leverage ratio, health/age depending. There are some companies that can offer up to 10 times or more, depending on your age and health.

So, in Jim and Lisa's case, they could take $100,000 for LTC expenses (instead of $200,000) and park it in an LTC annuity. Their benefit amount for care expenses could total $300,000 or more. And now, the best part is that their additional $100,000 is freed up to invest elsewhere – it has the potential to increase the value of the overall portfolio! Here's the reality: if they need care, they are going to spend the $300,000 anyways, out of their portfolio, so why not only spend $100,000 and get $200,000 guaranteed income-tax-free from the insurance companies?

Now, they have some level of portfolio insurance and less need to worry about how to pay for LTC expenses.

Again, everyone wins…but it gets even better.

Within the LTC annuities, there is still the opportunity to earn interest. So, the overall portfolio is growing there as well. Or the interest credited can be used to create more robust LTC coverage.

There are even options where the consumer and his or her spouse can receive **lifetime payments** while on claim. A couple can *never* outlive their benefits!

Let's look at another example to understand the mechanics:

Let's say Jim and Lisa purchase an LTC annuity for a lump sum payment of $100,000. And let's suppose their monthly benefit amount is $5,000. If either of them goes on claim, they will receive up to $5,000 per month. If both go on claim, they will receive $10,000 per month! All the funds received can be 100 percent income-tax-free.

As we can see, if both parties needed care, and they had no LTC insurance, the money would be gone in under a year. With a 3:1 leverage ratio, provided by LTC insurance, we now have *tripled* the length of coverage for the same price! And if we opt for the lifetime payment option, the policy has already paid for itself in 10 months' time, and they'll never have to worry about coverage again.

Other reasons to consider a long-term-care-focused annuity:

The health underwriting is generally less strenuous than it is for a life insurance policy. This is because on most long-term-care-focused annuities, there are no enhanced benefits if the insured passes away. The beneficiary will receive the remaining principal plus interest (minus any fees or withdrawals). However, there is no income-tax-free lump sum over and above that. The bottom line is that there's no life insurance, which means there's less risk for the insurance company. Therefore, they can offer these policies to those who might be less healthy.

Even if you are perfectly healthy and could qualify for life insurance, a long-term care annuity is still a viable option.

Let's look at an example in which we use qualified money (IRA, 401k, pension, etc.) to fund an LTCi policy:

Perhaps you have a portfolio that is heavily weighted in qualified money. If most of the funds are in an IRA, you are not able to move them into a life insurance policy unless you pay the taxes today! And for some, that may not make the most sense. However, with a long-term care annuity, you can move IRA money over into another IRA annuity that is focused on long-term care. There are no tax consequences to transfer from IRA to IRA. (There are only a couple companies that offer this type of long-term care annuity. Some of them may require you to de-qualify the lump sum over a period of time).

Another unique tax advantage to having a long-term care annuity can be captured by using a pre-existing annuity that you already own! The pre-existing annuity would need to be a non-qualified annuity (meaning not from an IRA), and then transferred into a long-term care annuity. Normally, with this type of annuity, you would pay taxes on the growth when you take distributions. However, if you move it into an annuity that is qualified for LTC and you use the distributions for qualified care, <u>you will never pay any income taxes!</u>

This is due to the Pension Protection Act that was passed in the early 2000s. Few people know about this, but it can be a great resource and help you dramatically with your long-term care planning.

Drawbacks:

But of course, nothing is perfect; there are some downsides to annuities as well:

No enhanced death benefit:

The long-term care benefits can be funded in many different ways with an annuity, but there is usually little to no enhancement of the death benefit, unlike life-insurance-based policies, where there is generally more death benefit. There is still a death benefit with LTC annuities that pay out to your beneficiary if you pass away, but the primary focus is on long-term care.

Funding requirements:

Annuities work best with a large lump sum payment up front. In fact, most annuity products have minimum funding requirements of $20,000 or more, depending on company, product, and tax status. If you don't yet have a large portfolio, the entry cost can be prohibitive. However, for folks who have earmarked funds for care, this is the perfect option to let your money do the work for you in a much more tax-efficient manner.

Lack of liquidity / surrender charge:

Annuities have a specified "surrender period" where there are penalties for early withdrawal of the money over certain limits. Long-term care annuities are built for long-term holding — not short-term. The specific details of the contract, including surrender values and limited liquidity need to be evaluated carefully before moving forward.

After the surrender period, you are free to do whatever you want with the money! (There are 100 percent liquid options on life-insurance-funded policies but have lower LTC benefit amounts, and most people don't exercise the liquidity feature.)

Conclusion:

We can remove some of the stink that's been placed on the word "annuity" in recent years. Rather, they can be a valuable tool to create leverage on your hard-earned money and mitigate the high costs of needing long-term care.

CHAPTER 13

TAX ADVANTAGES

Not only can the benefits of a long-term Care insurance policy be income-tax-free, but the premium payments can be tax deductible!

The premium payments on a life insurance policy are generally not deductible, because the benefit payment to the beneficiary is income-tax-free. A Roth IRA is not tax-deductible, because the value, plus any interest is income-tax-free (if you are following the rules for Roth). This is why long-term care insurance is unique. The government incentivizes individuals and businesses to hold long-term care insurance because it limits how much they may have to pay in the future. If you don't have any coverage and you've already gone through your assets, the government must come in and pay for it through Medicaid. It's funny how the tax code works; the government creates incentives through tax deductions and credits for programs they want to grow or spend less money on. There are also potential tax incentives for businesses and the owners of those businesses. If you are a business owner and have a corporation, you may be able to create a <u>100 percent tax deduction</u> when used to purchase qualified long-term care insurance! The business owner can also buy long-term care insurance on key employees.

Like anything else that's involved in the tax world, there are so many different variations, exclusions, and complexities. We are not going to get into all the various tax advantages, but these are just a few. Please consult with your CPA for actual tax advice.

CHAPTER 14

HANDLING SELF OBJECTIONS

1. **I'll self-insure: this *is* self-insurance** –every option is self-insurance, there are just better ways than others to create family protection, financial leverage, tax advantages, and options. As stated, the insurance companies are not handing out free insurance and ice cream cones. You must use your money, but in trade, they put up their money, too. Oftentimes, this can create two times, three times, four times, five times and even ten times the money for LTC. Quick example:

    E.g. $300,000 for care earmarked in the portfolio – let's use $100,000 with 3:1 leverage and invest the other $200,000 – allows higher risk tolerance for the remaining assets

    <u>This is a way to overcome your financial advisor's (fa) objections – e.g. the fa will now have more assets to manage *and* you will have ltc insurance = win win.</u> Think about, if you end up needing care, you are going to most likely spend the same $100,000 plus the other $200,000 that the insurance company was going to provide. If eligible both in terms of health and finances, why wouldn't you want to use $200,000 from the insurance company, income-tax-free?

But my financial advisor told me that I can self-insure

If we had a nickel…

We have learned that many financial advisors, with the best of intentions, will tell their clients that they can self-insure. But how many financial advisors or financial professionals do you know that would tell you to self-insure for your health insurance? Why would you sign up for Medicare and waste all that money on those premiums when you could self-insure? What about if your home is paid off? Would you still have homeowners' insurance? Start thinking about the things that you actually insure; cell phone, laptop, TV, etc. We're actually buying insurance on a lot of stuff that we could easily "self-insure," but when it comes to something that is statistically very likely to occur and we know that it is very expensive and can destroy family legacies, we don't even want to give it a second thought?

If this is the case for you or someone you know, simply ask your financial advisor/professional to put into writing that you can self-insure. Ask them to put it in an email. I think you know what happens next.

There are many reasons people are being advised that LTCi is not needed. But they mainly boil down to philosophy/lack of understanding.

Most financial advisors either
   a)   Are not aware of the LTC options available in today's marketplace
   b)   Are not certified/contracted to sell those products
   c)   Simply don't **want** to mess with the complex world of LTCi

Here's another way to think about it: run a portfolio analysis showing your average anticipated growth rate until you go to retire, or if you are retired, stretch it out until you are about age 80 then show a long-term care event. Have the event occur during a recession. Meaning have your portfolio depleted by a 20 percent market correction, and then you and your spouse withdrawing an additional $10,000 per month each or $20,000 total on top of what you are already withdrawing to pay for care. See how long your portfolio will last.

Ultimately, regardless of the advice you adhere to, the decisions you make today are going to affect you, your spouse, your kids/grandkids, and your overall legacy. Your financial advisor and insurance agent won't pay your bills in the future. This is another thing to ask your advisor if they are not providing LTCi options to you, "Will you pay the nursing home bill, in case assets are not able to cover it through your management?"

2. **It's too expensive, I cannot afford it, I saw online the premiums are really high, my friend told me that it's not worth the money.**

    Well, by this point, you can easily debunk these statements yourself. But this is a common hang-up that creates a lot of hesitation and lack of planning when it comes to long-term care. Whenever I hear, "This is too expensive" (before anyone has seen a quote), I ask the person, "How much is it?" The response is usually silence… Even if we see what the price is, let's ask ourselves if it's too expensive compared to the financial and emotional cost of needing long-term care. So, let's not assume that it's too expensive until we understand what the value is.

3. **I am not healthy enough; they would never take me.** This is another very common objection, but as we've reviewed, it may not be the case. At the time of writing this book, 2023, there are guaranteed long-term care plans. Yep, that's the right guaranteed issue, no matter what your health status is, you are eligible to have long-term care leverage. These plans may not be around forever, however, there are other options to create leverage that can help offset the costs of long-term care that may not specifically be long-term care insurance. This is a realm that we get into utilizing standard annuities, fixed and index to help create protection and leverage for not only the financial asset and retirement income, but also in the event of a long-term care situation for the family member. There are so many great options out there and unique opportunities that are not being discussed in the mainstream media or by most financial professionals. This is a unique niche in the financial world, asset protection, long-term care planning. Please do yourself a favor and your family a favor by at least exploring the options. If it's not for you, that's fine, at least you've done the homework to prove that. If you don't do the homework and later determine that it would have been good for you, but now, you're not eligible, that's going to be a very unfortunate realization and family conversation. Let's just think about this in reality: you're going to tell me that the majority of people who are currently receiving long-term care if they could go back in time to help get protection, they wouldn't do it? Don't be one of those people. At least know your options and make your own decision. Don't let somebody— i.e. a financial influencer—tell you that everything's going to be okay without any guarantees.

CHAPTER 15

GLOSSARY OF COMMON LONG-TERM CARE TERMINOLOGY

Activities of daily living (ADLs):
routine activities that people do every day without requiring assistance, including:
- bathing (getting into or out of a tub/shower)
- continence (maintaining control of bladder/bowel function)
- dressing (including any necessary braces or artificial limbs)
- eating (feeding yourself via utensils, feeding tube, or IV)
- toileting (getting on and off a toilet)
- transferring (from bed to chair, chair to bed, etc.)

Adult day care:
a local center that provides care and social services, which can allow caregivers to go to work or have a break from caregiving

Annuity:
an insurance contract in which one pays premium(s) and after a period, money is paid to payee(s) each year for a set period or for the rest of their lives

Assisted living facility:
a housing facility for people who don't require more in-depth care provided in a nursing home

Bed reservation:
a benefit that reserves the insured's accommodations in a long-term care facility if they require hospitalization while confined

Beneficiary:
a person eligible to receive proceeds from a life insurance policy

Benefit period:
the length of time during which a benefit is paid (months, years, or lifetime)

Care coordination services:
the organization of care activities for an individual to facilitate the appropriate delivery of long-term care services

Caregiver:
someone who helps another person accomplish activities of daily living due to an illness, injury, or severe cognitive impairment

Caregiver training:
training for an unpaid, informal caregiver to care for an insured at home

Cash surrender value:
the amount offered to the policy owner upon cancellation of a life insurance or annuity contract, which is the cash value minus any fees or costs

Chronically ill:
someone unable to perform two of six activities of daily living for a period of at least 90 days, or who requires substantial supervision due to severe cognitive impairment

Daily benefit:
the maximum amount a long-term care insurance plan will pay in a single day

Death benefit:
the amount paid to a beneficiary upon the death of an insured person

Elimination period (also known as waiting period):
a set number of days an insured is required to pay his or her long-term care costs before benefits are paid

Guaranteed interest rate:
the rate at which your cash value is increased annually, guaranteed for the life of your contract at the time of purchase

Guaranteed single premium:
the option to fund a policy or annuity with a single lump sum amount

Home health aide:
a trained, certified professional who can be hired to visit individuals in their own home to provide help with activities of daily living

Home healthcare:
a wide range of care services like assistance with activities of daily living, respite care, maintenance and personal care services received at home

Home modification:
Updating a house to make it more suitable to the resident, which may include installing a wheelchair ramp, walk-in tub, or grab bars

Homemaker services:
nonmedical, nominal support services provided by a professional or volunteer that can help a person to remain at home, including meal preparation, laundry, cleaning and supervising self-administration of medicine

Hospice:
specially designed to provide care and support, with a focus on comfort and not treatment, toward the end of life

Issue age:
the age of an insured as of the date a policy is issued

Joint issue age:
in insurance and annuity contracts with two insureds, a calculated age based on the age of both insureds as a means to rate the lives as one

Licensed healthcare practitioner:
any physician, any registered professional nurse or licensed social worker, or other individual who meets such requirements as may be prescribed by the U.S. Secretary of the Treasury, excluding any member of your immediate family

Long-term care:
a myriad of medical and social services designed to support the needs of chronically ill individuals

Modified Endowment Contract (MEC):
a tax qualification of a life insurance policy with cash value where the policy has been funded with more money than allowed under federal law

Monthly benefit:
the maximum amount a long-term care insurance policy will pay in a single month

Nursing home:
a residential facility that offers accommodations and is equipped and staffed to provide personal or nursing care for persons unable to care for themselves

Plan of care:

a formal plan prescribed by a licensed health care practitioner tailored to meet an individual's needs regarding qualified long-term care services

Policy:

a legal contract written by an insurance company and issued to a policy owner or group sponsor to define the benefits the company is required to pay

Policy loan:

a loan issued by an insurance company that utilizes the cash value in a life policy as collateral

Policy owner:

the individual who has a legal, signed contract with the insurance provider

Power of Attorney (POA):

a legal document that grants authority for another person to make decisions on another's behalf, most often related to medical treatment and living arrangements

Return of premium:

a benefit that allows you to surrender your contract and receive the premium you've paid less any withdrawals or prior distributions

Severe cognitive impairment:
when a person has trouble remembering, learning new things, concentrating or making decisions that affect their everyday life or loss of safety awareness

Single premium deferred annuity (SPDA):
an annuity contract purchased with a single lump-sum of money that pays only after a specified amount of time has elapsed

Single premium immediate annuity (SPIA):
an annuity contract purchased with a single lump-sum of money and in exchange begins paying almost immediately

Supportive equipment: includes installation fees, labor, and related costs an insured might incur for the purchase or rental of supportive equipment

Surrender charges:
a charge for early withdrawal of funds from an insurance or annuity contract, or cancellation of the contract

Underwriting:
the process of using non-medical, medical, or health information in the evaluation of an applicant for insurance coverage

Underwriting classes:
a group of individuals with similar characteristics used to determine the premium that should be charged for coverage

REFERENCES

2015 Alzheimer's disease facts and figures. (2015, March 1). Alzheimer's Association. Retrieved February 4, 2023, from https://alz-journals.onlinelibrary.wiley.com/doi/10.1016/j.jalz.2015.02.003

Evercare & National Alliance for Caregiving. (2006, September). *Evercare Study of Caregivers in Decline, National Association of Caregiving.* Caregivers.org. Retrieved February 4, 2023, from https://www.caregiving.org/wp-content/uploads/2020/05/Caregivers-in-Decline-Study-FINAL-lowres.pdf

How Much Care Will You Need? | ACL Administration for Community Living. (n.d.). https://acl.gov/ltc/basic-needs/how-much-care-will-you-need

National Nursing Home Survey. (2015, November 6). Centers for Disease Control and Prevention. Retrieved February 4, 2023, from https://www.cdc.gov/nchs/nnhs/index.htm?CDC_AA_refVal=https%3A%2F%2Fwww.cdc.gov%2Fnchs%2Fnnhs.htm

Schulz, R., Mendelsohn, A. B., Haley, W. E., Mahoney, D., Allen, R. S., Zhang, S., Thompson, L., & Belle, S. H. (2013). *End-of-life care and the effects of bereavement on family caregivers of persons with dementia.* Retrieved February 4, 2023, from https://pubmed.ncbi.nlm.nih.gov/14614169/

Schulz, R., PhD. (2001, June 27). *Involvement in Caregiving and Adjustment to Death of a Spouse : Findings From the Caregiver Health Effects.* https://jamanetwork.com/journals/jama/fullarticle/193954

Seniorliving.org. (2023, January 10). *Nursing Home Costs in 2023.* SeniorLiving.org. https://www.seniorliving.org:443/nursing-homes/costs/

Whiting, C. G., Heinz, P. A., Wittke, M. R., Reinhard, S., Feinberg, L. F., Skufca, L., Stephen, R., & Choula, R. (2020, November). *Caregiving in the U.S. 2020: A Focused Look at Family Caregivers of Adults Age 50+.* Caregiving.org. Retrieved February 4, 2023, from https://www.caregiving.org/wp-content/uploads/2021/05/AARP1340_RR_Caregiving50Plus_508.pdf

www.ingramcontent.com/pod-product-compliance
Lightning Source LLC
LaVergne TN
LVHW011853060526
838200LV00054B/4315